P9-AFI-455

MY TOUR of EUROPE
By Teddy Roosevelt, Age 10

osevelt, Theodore,
tour of Europe : by
ddy Roosevelt, age 10 /
003.
3052044641113
07/21/03

MY TOUR of EUROPE
By Teddy Roosevelt, Age 10

Edited by Ellen Jackson

Illustrated by Catherine Brighton

THE MILLBROOK PRESS   BROOKFIELD, CONNECTICUT

SANTA CLARA COUNTY LIBRARY

3 3305 20446 4113

To Jean Reynolds, with thanks

Library of Congress Cataloging-in-Publication Data
Roosevelt, Theodore, 1858–1919.
[Diaries. Selections]
My tour of Europe : by Teddy Roosevelt, age 10 / edited by Ellen Jackson ; illustrated by Catherine Brighton.
p. cm.
Summary: Presents illustrated excerpts from the journal kept by ten-year-old Theodore Roosevelt as his family toured Europe.
ISBN 0-7613-2516-6 (lib. bdg.)
1. Roosevelt, Theodore, 1858-1919—Childhood and youth—Juvenile literature. 2. Roosevelt, Theodore, 1858-1919—Journeys—Europe—Juvenile literature. 3. Roosevelt, Theodore, 1858-1919—Diaries—Juvenile literature. 4. Presidents—United States—Diaries—Juvenile literature. 5. Europe—Description and travel—Juvenile literature. [1. Roosevelt, Theodore, 1858-1919—Childhood and youth. 2. Roosevelt, Theodore, 1858-1919—Journeys—Europe. 3. Roosevelt, Theodore, 1858-1919—Diaries. 4. Presidents—Diaries. 5. Europe—Description and travel.] I. Jackson, Ellen B., 1943– II. Brighton, Catherine, ill. III. Title.
E757 .A3 2002   973.91'1'092—dc21   2002008949

Copyright © 2003 by Ellen Jackson
Illustrations copyright © 2003 by Catherine Brighton
All rights reserved.

The editor would like to thank Wallace Finley Dailey, Curator of
the Theodore Roosevelt Collection in the Harvard College Library
and Dr. John Gable of the Theodore Roosevelt Association
for their invaluable assistance in providing access
to Theodore Roosevelt's diaries.

Diary excerpts are from the Theodore Roosevelt Collection,
Harvard College Library, and are used by permission of the Houghton Library,
Harvard University (*43M-818 nos. 2-6) and by permission of
The Theodore Roosevelt Association, Oyster Bay, New York.

Published by The Millbrook Press, Inc.
2 Old New Milford Road
Brookfield, Connecticut 06804
www.millbrookpress.com

Printed in the United States of America
1 3 5 4 2

Editor's Note

Theodore Roosevelt, the twenty-sixth president of the United States, was a great leader who wanted to make life better for the American people. All his life, Theodore Roosevelt loved nature and the outdoors. Before he was president, Roosevelt was a cowboy, soldier, and hunter. As president, he set aside land for national forests and created the first forest ranger stations.

Theodore Roosevelt was a busy president, but he knew how to have fun, too. When Roosevelt was in the White House, his six children were often seen laughing and running up and down the halls while the president chased them pretending to be a bear. Sometimes Roosevelt would join them in a pillow fight.

The journal you are about to read was written by Theodore Roosevelt when he was a boy. When Theodore was ten, his mother and father took the family to Europe for a year. As the family toured Europe, Theodore wrote in his journal, describing the places he visited and the fun he had with his brother, Ellie, and sister Conie. (Theodore's older sister, Bamie, was considered one of the "grown-ups.")

Like most children, Theodore wasn't always interested in what the grown-ups were doing. Theodore had asthma, and often he was sick. Sometimes he got into trouble.

Theodore did not spell every word in his journal correctly. The words he misspelled have been corrected to make the journal easier to read. You will find a list of these corrections at the back of the book.

Did Theodore Roosevelt imagine that he would grow up to be president? Probably not. In many ways, he was just like any other ten-year-old boy.

But Theodore did know how to work hard—and how to play hard, too.

Perhaps there is a boy or girl reading this book right now who will grow up to be president. Could it be you?

May 16, 1869 (at sea)
While lying in bed with nothing to do I got so, so, homesick.

May 17, 1869 (Still at sea)
Clear, calm and cold. We saw two ships and a great many fish.

May 29, 1869 (Liverpool, England)
We all went with our cousins to Southport and had a ride on donkeys. We had great fun for they galloped so funnily and it was so nice. In jumping over a fence I cut my leg a good deal.

June 14, 1869
(York, England)
Conie and I went alone to the museum where we saw birds and skeletons and Bamie and I went in for a spree and got two shillings worth of rock candy.

July 10, 1869 (London, England)
We all went to the tower of London. A kind man dressed like an ancient warden showed us round...I put my head on the block where so many had been beheaded.

July 15, 1869 (Antwerp, Belgium)
We went to the botanic gardens and played at wild bears and hunting and being hunted.

July 31, 1869 (Jura, Switzerland)
Early in the morning Conie and I went out and climbed round on a bank and picked a lot of wildflowers which we gave to Papa and Mama.

August 6, 1869 (Chamonix, France)
We explored the hotel (Conie, Ellie, and I) and met with several cross chambermaids.

August 18, 1869 (Switzerland)
We went to the top of the Agishorn. We snowballed each other and walked in the snow and were cold as could be...

August 23, 1869 (Switzerland
We had our hair cut and
went shopping in the mornin
and in the afternoon we
played in the house, threw
paper balls at waiter and
chambermaid and rushed
around upstairs and
downstairs to dodge them.

August 29, 1869
I was very sick on the sofa
and lay in bed all day and
had to take arrowroot.
Mama told me stories and
Papa did the same.

September 9, 1869 (near the border
of Switzerland and Italy)
I sat with one leg in Italy and the other in Switzerland.

September 13, 1869 (near the border of Switzerland and Italy)
We played in the garden and then rowed on Lake Lugano by
the light of a silver moon. Half our way was in Italy half in
Switzerland.

October 11, 1869 (Bavaria, Germany)
I went out with the three big people and the other two children stayed at the hotel. We 4 went first to the royal palace. We saw the private chapel of the king, his state room and throne and the gilded bronze statues.

October 22, 1869 (Berlin, Germany)
We all (big people too) went to the dentist. The others had their teeth filled which took a long while and I had one pulled which took a few seconds.

November 3, 1869 (Paris, France)
We took a walk and had a stick of candy and once we went on a kind of circus where we got on wooden horses (hung to long poles which were on a big one) which were pushed round...

November 4, 1869 (Paris, France)
We saw the Triumphal Arch and had ice cream. Papa, Mama, and Bamie went out to dinner. I think Paris splendid though sunny France is very rainy...

November 25, 1869
The doctor came to me today and for the 3d time changed all my medicines. I lay down most of the time. I have no appetite but can drink tea and eat toast the doctor says.

December 16, 1869 (Genoa, Italy)
It was dark as pitch when Ellie and I began to jump. This woke Conie.
She came in. We got noisy. We jumped about pulled the covering off
the bed and kicked and made an awful noise. Then Father came and
made us quiet.

December 19, 1869 (Pisa, Italy)
We were awake at 6 but did not get up until half past 7. We all went to
church. After church we went to the leaning tower and the cathedral.
The tower leans 13 feet and looks all the time as if it would fall.

December 21, 1869 (On the way to Rome by train) We are now at another station. We all got out and we saw a beautiful big huge dog and I was the only one he shook hands with and I am proud...

December 25, 1869
Christmas! Christmas!
hip, hip, hurrah! ... I was
awake at 4 and we all 4
children got up at a little
before 6 and went in to
Mama's and Papa's bed...
We then opened our
stockings. They were nice
and bulky... I had a
compass, thermometer, 19
photographs, a cardinal's
cap. A pair of gloves and
a beautiful cravat...

December 29, 1869
(Naples, Italy)
The sun was shining in a blue sky when we got up and before we were dressed it was raining. We have rooms on the bay of Naples and in sight of Vesuvius the last with a little smoke and a little snow on the top of it.

January 9, 1870 (Rome, Italy)
In a park we met an American boy and played with him leap frog over some posts and invited him to dinner at Thursday.

February 26, 1870 (Florence, Italy)
We played in the garden making roads of stones and city and palaces and catacombs. We then saw the zoological gardens where the monkeys were so funny and the wolves howled a great deal. The geese bit. We played in the garden again. We then had a play fight. With soldiers.

March 13, 1870 (Paris, France) We went to church... Going home it snowed and blew so that my umbrella blew away and we had a long chase after it.

March 15, 1870 (Paris, France)
Ice on the fountain. Sailed our boats in cracks in it... Ellie and I played bear and hunter in the trees of the Tuileres garden.

May 24, 1870 (At sea on the way back to America)
In the afternoon we saw some young whales one of whom came so near the boat that when it spouted some of its water came on me.

May 25, 1870 (home)
New York!!! Hip! Hurrah!

Keeping a Journal

Theodore Roosevelt described his trip to Europe in his journal. Journals can include many different kinds of information and stories. Here are some tips to help you begin a journal of your own:

■ Even if you haven't traveled to exciting places as Theodore Roosevelt did, you can find many interesting things in your life to write about. Below is a list of possible topics. Write down any other ideas you may have and keep this list with your journal. Refer to it whenever you have trouble thinking of a topic:

daily weather
family history
pets
indoor games
school
sports
food
dreams
crafts and hobbies
feelings
future plans
poems and stories

- Read stories about Paul Bunyan and make up a "tall tale" about your family, your school, or your friends.

- What is your favorite color, book, song, story, place?

- What kind of people do you like to have as friends? If you could make a wish for someone else (not you) what would it be?

- Theodore Roosevelt was president of the United States one hundred years ago. In those days many homes did not have indoor plumbing. Very few people had automobiles. Television and airplanes were unknown.

  Someday the people of the twenty-second century will want to know about life in the twenty-first century. Imagine that you are in charge of selecting items for a time capsule. Choose ten items that will tell the people of the future about your life in the twenty-first century. Why did you choose each one? Write about your choices in your journal.

- It's fun to go sightseeing, but it's also fun to explore imaginary places. Pretend that you have just returned from the planet Zooranus. On Zooranus you explored the planet and chose an animal to bring back to Earth as a pet. Describe your new pet. What does it look like? What does it eat? Where does it live on its native planet? Is it dangerous? Are there any problems in keeping it at your house?

- Theodore Roosevelt loved the outdoors. He often wrote about the plants and animals he observed. Is there an empty lot, an overgrown field, or other left-alone place in your neighborhood? Collect gifts from nature. One good way to collect hidden insects is to place a box or white piece of paper under a branch of a tree and shake the branch. You can also collect rocks, feathers, and other treasures from your special place. Write about what you observe or find.

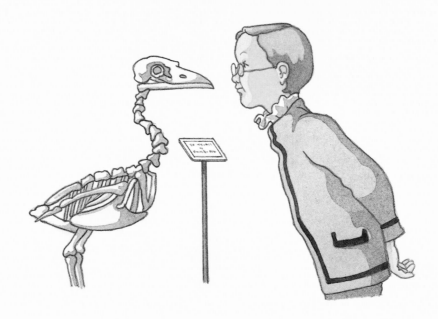

About Theodore Roosevelt

■ Theodore Roosevelt's nickname was Teddy. While he was president, a popular children's toy was named after him. Can you guess what toy it was?

■ Theodore Roosevelt is one of four presidents who is honored at the Mount Rushmore National Monument in South Dakota. Do you know the names of the other presidents whose faces appear there?

■ Theodore Roosevelt became president in 1901. How has life changed since 1901? Can you think of five things that would surprise Theodore Roosevelt about life in the United States today?

Notes on Spelling

In this journal, Theodore Roosevelt misspelled some simple words, such as *maney* and *citty*. But he also spelled some long words, such as *chambermaids* and *Switzerland*, correctly.

When he became president, Theodore Roosevelt wanted to make English words easier to spell by adopting a plan called Simplified Spelling. If he had succeeded, the word photograph would now be spelled *fotograf*. Can you guess why? Which hard-to-spell words would you like to change?

The following are words that Theodore Roosevelt spelled incorrectly in this journal:

May 16 - lying spelled **lieing**
May 17 - many spelled **maney**
June 14 - skeletons spelled **skeletens**
June 28 - Hyde Park not capitalized, waxworks spelled **wax works,** several spelled **severel**
July 7 - Crystal Palace spelled **christal palace**
July 10 - many spelled **maney**
July 31 - Early spelled **Earley**, wildflowers spelled **wild flowers**
August 23 - shopping spelled **shoping**
September 13 - Lake not capitalized, way spelled **waw**
October 11 - statues spelled **statutes**
October 20 - Natural History Museum not capitalized, animals spelled **analels**
October 22 - dentist capitalized
November 4 - Triumphal Arch spelled **triumphel arch**, very spelled **verry**

November 25 - doctor spelled **docter**, appetite spelled **appitiet**
December 16 - awful spelled **offul**
December 19 - until spelled **untill**, half past spelled **halfpast**
December 25 - Mama's and Papa's punctuated **Mamas** and **Papas**, bulky spelled **bulkey**, compass spelled **compas**, cardinal's spelled **cardinel's**, thermometer spelled **themometer**,
December 29 - dressed spelled **dresed**, Vesuvius spelled **Vesuvious**
January 9 - American, Thursday not capitalized
February 26 - city spelled **citty**, zoological spelled **zooological**, wolves spelled **wolfs**, soldiers spelled **soilders**
March 13 - away spelled **a way**
March 15 - Tuileries spelled **tuileres**

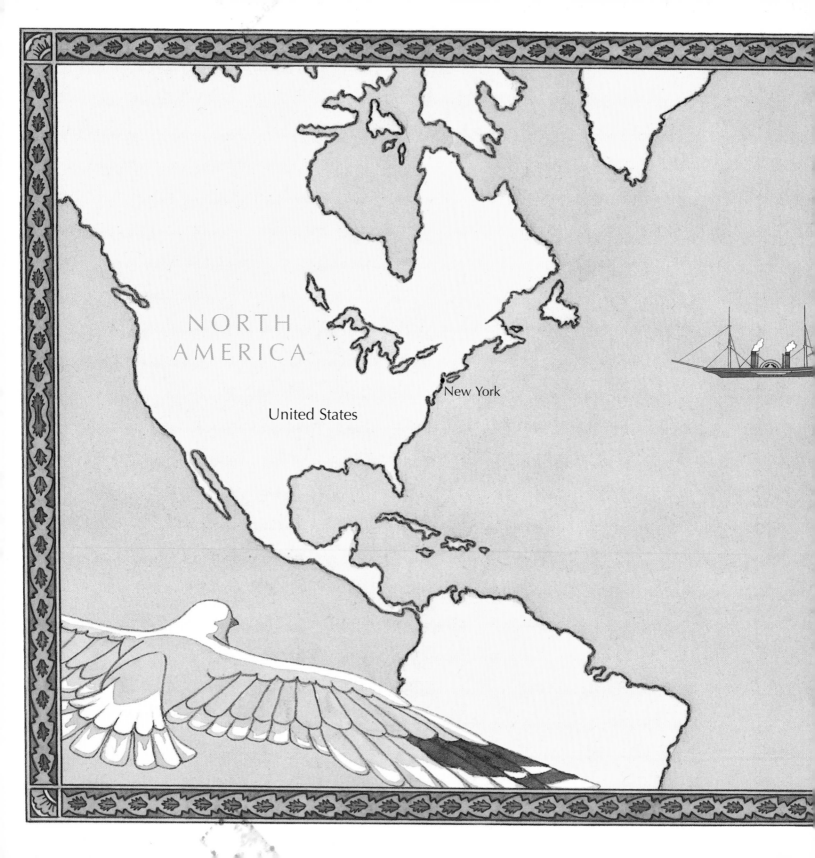

NORTH
AMERICA

United States

New York